AR:RANGE:MENTS

ESTHER KONDO HELLER

Fonograf Editions
Portland, OR

Cover design and typesetting by Mike Corrao

First Edition, First Printing

FONO35

Published by Fonograf Editions
www.fonorafeditions.com

Distributed by NYU Press
NYUPress.org

[clmp]

Fonograf Editions is a proud member of the Community of Literary Magazines and Presses

ISBN: 978-1-964499-39-0
ISBN (ebook): 978-1-964499-41-3
ISBN (library ed. hardcover): 978-1-964499-40-6
LCCN: 2024946091

AR:RANGE:MENTS

FONOGRAF EDITIONS

CONTENTS

for Zipora

I: REMEMBER

The word of *remember (re-member)* evokes the coming
together of severed parts, fragments becoming a whole.

—bell hooks

In school, writing was called composition.
Something with a beginning and a body
growing to conclude.
                              —THE END

I remembered her every day
although she long dead
never saw her body
still hear fragments of her poetry
in major/minor scales
cyclic episodes of holding her
carrying her round
the length of every arc I write
tangents to some other
memory spilling to another-
other in the perimeter of another

touch her here w/out beginning/end

drawing circles to fetch non-cyclical words
w'out a ladder channelling

to gather ⊆ arrange⊆ utterance ⊆ translation⊆
of holy language⊆
silence⊆ dying⊆ change⊆
composting⊆ breath⊆ spirit
⊆ transpire ⊆ pass-through water

I imagine being in the city with you sometimes now, Mama, us holding hands, me telling you some random fact about a place where the ice cream is good, you ask me something

. . .   something

I looked

for you in   *News From*
Home,   although
you could   not have
been there   during filming
in 1977.   I am
looking for   an

arrangement, I know that you made arrangements —I hear them in the conch,
the ocean, in the static, the silence   of your holy arrangement followed by
every utterance

I am looking for image and text arrangements-

there   are many moving combinations of image and text that tense time and tell

of the otherwise possible, sound out a memory of understanding.

to be

One time, while walking under the trees and watching the shapes formed between the almost touching trees, in that almost touching space, I heard May Ayim say, I want to be understood   I want to be understood

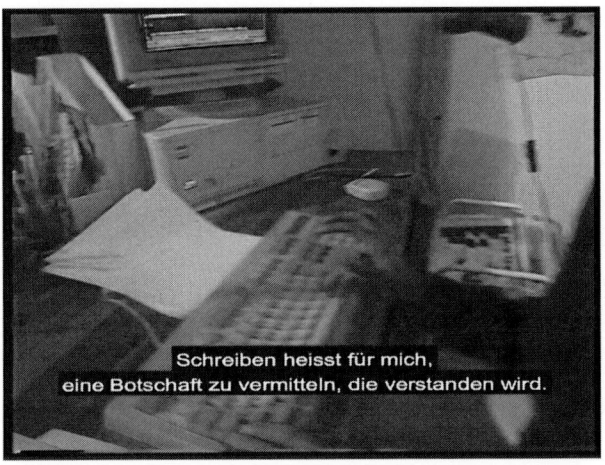

Schreiben heisst für mich,
eine Botschaft zu vermitteln, die verstanden wird.

I want to be understood

I want

o

o

d

tiefe Wunderung
in der befinde ich
mich im mich
dort im Schnitt der
wunde rung
wunder ich mich
über das ich
zwischen gedicht
ich stehe in der
Sprachlichkeit
im Rachen die
Verbindung zwischen
den Mundraum
und den luft raum
im rachen dort liege ich
das kratzende Kind
dessen Körper sprach
in Genauigkeit in dem es
sich aufriss zu wunden
meine Haut vertrocknete
Maji Maji verdunstet
in keine Sprache
überall Blutwunder

damu yangu ina zugunka
                    roho yangu
kama maji
                    roho yangu
kama upepo
                    huwezi kusau
damu yangu
                    iko kila
mahali   kila mahali

When my mother was dying, she spoke English. It was her dying language. She did not want me to understand what she was saying on her deathbed. I did not speak English yet, but my father would say to her, *You know she can understand you, they have English lessons now.* Then he'd turn to me and say, *Show your Mama some of your English.*

Hello, how are you?

My name is...

I love you

I love you

I love you

I love you

I I... you

I love you

My mama would mutter things in English but I remember only a single utterance: No.... No.... No.... No.... No....

[silence]

In linguistics, utterances are units of speech that are followed by silence. When she died all I said was... [   ]

What is wrong?

Nothing, I
m[utter].

In the word 'mutter', there is at once my mother and the silence.
Mut:ter.

Clap your hands twice

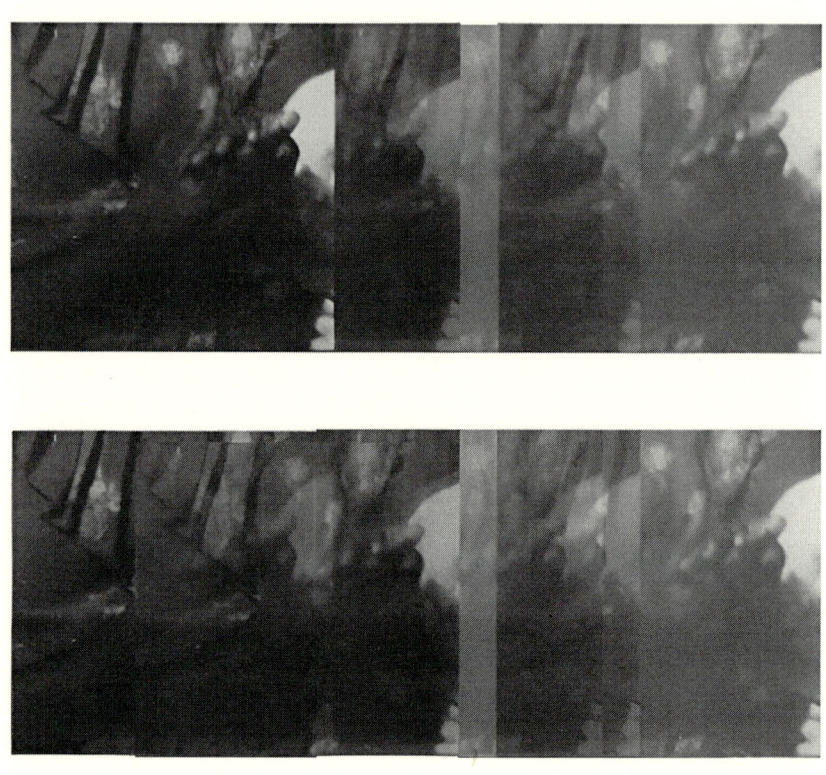

Clap your hands twice

Clapping.
Clapping.
Clapping.
Clapping.
Clapping.
Clapping.
Clapping.

silence

An
opening is

a leaking basket
holding some
things together

MAD SHINY

On Sunday we wrestled. I curled my body into the drawer. Mama's voice caught me and threw me out. My legs dragged along the carpet floor, tears rolling down my face, my father laughed somewhere in the corner, betting all his money on another family. I fall to the pillow that rests on the floor between my mother's legs. She holds my head and leans my neck to the right. I rest my head against her thigh. Her fingers search for knots to loosen on my head. I make a noise and move. She hisses, *hold still.* Then reaches for the comb and starts to brush. Wrestling is a performance. I know my role and cry, scream, and kick in the air. *That child is crazy, that child is crazy,* I want them to say crazy again call me crazy. *No child of mine is going to school looking crazy.* She puts her hand on my shoulder and tells me that she won't tell me to be still again.

On Sunday we fought.
But every Sunday I slept
mad shiny mad shiny

A front yard is a state of mind
the state of this mind thinks

about outdated maps
there is no porch in this dream

no picket fences perhaps
long stretches of sand

clay soil wringing the roots
of all water, all that's left is

structure crisp white clean
like your dad's church shirts

the only thing he tended to
with all his attention and care

sometimes he would starch
your shirt to teach you how

to cover your straight back
in the narrow fabric pressed

warm by his hands that do
not hold you now—been un

held since you could walk
I met you stumbling on a fenceless

lawn your face buried in the ground
gnashing your teeth into the

springs of the folds of my mind's
mattress uncovered on the floor

that winter when the boiler burst
and we were cold but alive and decent

If erasure is a reconsideration of a text or an image, then who do I reconsider in the archive? The bus is an archive of bodies, it contains a newspaper that has been left for us to complete the crossword. A train holds prints exposed and unexposed, I walk into the A train one afternoon and watch a woman crack a hardboiled egg open on the rail. She peels the shell, pulls a small saltshaker out of her bag, and salts the egg to her liking… she eats it and gets off at the next stop. I am no longer on the train but I think about the sound of the tapping egg again. I go to the archive to reconsider, to meddle, to not mind my own business because I mind, I do not alter.

///

Incomplete
A sentence
Leave it open

> with
> pondering
> ellipses
> . . .
> that leaks more than just
> me and my interior rhythm

. . .

II: DWELLING

It's as if you get there and home gets up and leaves and you have to go chase it. It keeps moving on.

That's the kind of agitation and wandering spirit that runs through the poems.

—Nathaniel Mackey

March 20, 1848. I dreamed that Rebecca Perot and I were in a house upon a rock together, and a storm arose, which made us feel that we were in great danger. A storm arose also in the west, and both met together and came with great force upon the house. A stream of water ran north and south upon the east side of the house. And I thought the storm would dash the house into the water and it would carry us down to New York, and then our friends would see our good home, and our destruction also. I felt not to go out, and I said to Rebecca, "We will stay in the house," though the storm was heavy. And the house stood firm, because it was on a rock. [WR 105]

-Rebecca Cox Jackson

Rebecca is in the river   I feel her skin in this sweet water

      stroking her without latching on to her   :desire: longing to be

         the water never asked   where we are going

            the water cleans my hands

    spooling pearls: whisper breath: mist dedications into minute openings

      moist visions that swell the banks where river flowers grow

lobelias purge us of that which does not let our weeds grow

Rebecca is dreaming   :pulsating: water:

unafraid like sunlight splaying dandelions open

R.P appears *aplunging* in the river   where they can be

         in the flesh   holding hands

      Rebecca stood... I stand admiring R.P coming and going

  in her undergarments facing Rebecca out of the water going

    further into the creek that feeds this dream to grow

blue and orange   westward-facing windows that burn hands

  on hot afternoons swells skin contains water

    this dream is not a window it is a house to be

coming out in   :peeled: intact: open

On the north side of the creek,   I open

                              the door to the house that asks me when I am going

to get out of those pants   lick pomegranate honey off the marble counter be

-cause there is no television watching   all my books are borrowed I grow

        hoarded words on my tongue in this house not home with hot running water

a stove top to melt jars of butter: infuse the oil with cedar: glaze my organs with bare hands

            lather dandelion orifices   I dream of oscillating hands

        on my back   what if the act of dreaming is not open?

Rebecca documents her dream of living together in a house upon a rock by a stream of water

            east side of the house her dream lessons a storm that is going

    to dash the house into the water carrying us down to New York to grow

    our good home on another rock close to friends but this house dashing wind will be

    the uncovering of our home's destruction   so the dream tells us to stay be

    Rebecca says "we will stay in the house"   reaches out her hands

                                        As the storm grows

heavy their: my: this house stands firm on the rock my/her/their dream instructs me to open

                                    all windows the wind is going

                            to swallow me whole with/in/out: saltwater

                            dash me where the river hands

their mouth to the ocean   in this dream   all my mothers

grow

                    perpetually present   her: them: me: conspiring

                                                                    to be

going
hands

speckled face spectacular
fire works in mysterious
wandering hands
circle of fire signs
flickering eyes meet
here for the first time
in this burning
peace/home here
dove's laughter fills
concrete   blue dances
to only woman d.j with degree
sounding out of the soundsystem
the orange flame
dubbed in the kisses
to come –
the burning
coil resting on the mouth
of a coke bottle staining glass
to a sticky note still

my mind is a barking dog
named Denzel by a woman
that has never cooked in her
life but always has something
to say about the stew to tomato
paste ratio it's always too much paste
never enough stew, but alas, she always
finishes the too much tomato paste stew
only leaves a sucked-clean bone for
Denzel is digging a hole in my medulla
oblongata system pulls out two snakes
one digs their fangs into his throat
the other spits venom into his spine
Denzel spins in slow motion to the
song of the enchanted sea yodelling
German shepherd in the valley
of my pituitary foaming at the mouth
before you fall, you gaze at the gramophone
horn in the soil that played the writhing
snake song that stopped your beating
heart. In the morning, a wheelbarrow scoops you up
the woman that named you eats cocoa puffs
with hot frothed milk, she says she never liked
that dog always pissing and jumping everywhere

1993-2001

2001-2005

From the ages of 8 - 12, I would go outside during
the full moon. Lie on my back and reflect on her
lessons: do your h/w, brush your teeth, moisturize
the backs of your knees, translate your anger.

2001-2006

Wavelengths, that I shed and drowned my lungs in on
the day when you died. Your son who loves that radio
says, don't cry mama would not want us to cry.

2001- 2020

She never visited me   in all my loneliness she never visited me   she let me sit with myself and said hold yourself and I am holding you   hold yourself and I am holding you hold yourself

I am holding

2020- 2020

My mama visited me in a dream for the first time, as
a laughing child. In the dream, I looked at my face in
the mirror, and when I noticed the child's eyes look-
ing at me, irritated I chased the child out of the room.
She ran out of the house, and I followed her giggles,
till she turned and there in her arms, she was, my
mother grown and whole - baby I love you, you did as
I said, laid those baby hairs to rest wrapped in satin
sheets every night moisturized baby
　　　I love you I love you I love me I love you…

Where are you going?

2001 - 2020

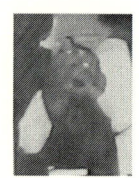

I saw my mother; she came to me in a dream.
I had never seen her so whole since,
her passing. She visited me seven days before the day
that would mark nineteen years since her death.
In the dream she was happy to see me, there was nothing
about her that translated to disappointment or sadness.

She asked me to consider
Where was I going to be at home?
What about Berlin…

Where will you rest truly?

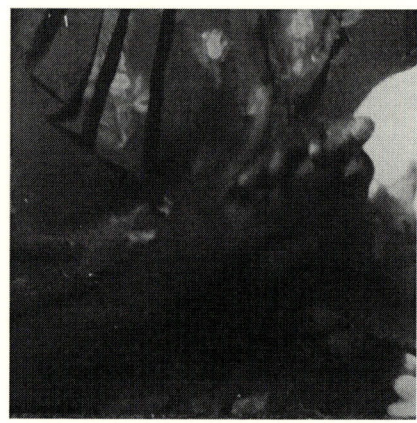

2001 -

Dark blue speckled cup by Mama's bedside,
pools her saliva pools Mama's words.

In every city I look for that cup and never buy
it hold it to my mouth
...

What is this seed of language? I am writing here in English, a language that M. NourbeSe Philip calls a foreign anguish. There is a cold-hard and swollen fruit I am pressing to my mouth to carry its pods with me in the pocket of my gums, in the gaps of my teeth, in that space where I am missing a tooth. My mama's passing on my lips.

A note in my book reads: I needed to find a language for speaking as a Black woman, whose Black mother died.

What does it mean to be whole? My mouth is a black hole, that I have tried to speak through in whatever language is needed, since she died. I have poured into it with anguish, seeds, my mother's brown leather watch, a piece of my dancing body, a mortared snail, honey, textures, script, fabric, Chaka Khan's "I feel for you," backbone, marrow, magnolia, sunflower, hibiscus, plumeria, foam, poetry, tree ...

What nail will I use?
To knot my tongue's verses.

in the day the girl who dreamt
on her maker's bed

packed a bag to abort herself from
this home that carried shells of her

mother's womb hoping to disappear

        under the shade of the tree listened

        to the birds stayed silent to
        hear her heartbeat pushing softly

        against the cold white wall to listen
        to leather catch skin   slipping

        out of this home into a tree
        whose arms are always open
        saves her

        voice for the ants whispers her
        dreams for them to feed to the
ungrieved

        hoping they bless   always hoping
they bless

III: COMPOSITIONS

As I began developing parts out of pieces, I found that I preferred them unconnected - to be related but not to touch - to circle, not line up, because the story of this prayer was the story of a shattered splintered life. The novel turned out to be a composition of parts circling one another, like the galaxy accompanying memory.

—Toni Morrison

WATER WALKER: OCEAN ARRANGEMENTS

trust the ocean

to sing me a lullaby
in my mother's tongue

trust the ocean

to let me take a hit of her salt-preserved
ashes when I surrender
 to her waves that wash
over me every full moon
trust the ocean to call

me

to

call

me

call

me

call

me

call

me

call

me

call

me

home

I trust the ocean to tell me about each grain of sand that has traces of skin

word of foam   where are you from?
word of foam   where are you from?
word of foam   where are you from?

you're mouthing off somewhere in the coral
my moan touches every stone every pebble
carries another me out of   sand
wind tones through the horn   language pools
in the dunes of lips trying to speak   mourn
froths from constant agitation every word
aerated longwinded speech patterns
the mystery of my story mystery of my story
         cackles in the fire of to be burnt files
as ordered by never my majesty to only be handled
by officers of european descent only
spirited away documents in oil drums my brother
The wind spreads static notes in the smoke transferring
from one lung to another to

from?
coral
pebble
sand

from?
from?
from?

coral
pebble
sand
pools
mourn
word
patterns
story
files
handled
only
brother
smoke
to

pools

mourn

word

patterns

story

files

pools

mourn

word

story

Files

pools

Files

word

mourn

that is how the neighbors saw the smoke

my mama cleaned the windows with newspaper til
there was not a single print left on the glass

my baby brother was burning books to boil an egg
in the living room   I was in a dream adorned in laterite

when I heard the screams
then the smell of melted plastic charred book spines

smoke rising from a burnt hole of one of the sofa
set pillows   my sister shapes words through the window

that we are fine no need to call the fire brigade the fire has ceased
the neighbors the same ones my mother would greet with

a smile to no response or slammed doors had already dialed
to extinguish the crisis but to their dismay we did not move

rent was paid on time only the carpet had converged forming
a crater no a mouth no a black hole in the ground

I never heard my parents argue behind the closed living room
door   their hushed voices inhaled by the burnt hole

newspaper
glass
smoke
burning
laterite
screams
spines
sofa
windows
ceased
with
dialed
move
forming
ground
room
hole
surface
sinks

glass

smoke

burning

laterite

screams

spines

windows

ceased

with

dialed

move

Not all land/papers were(are) torched to ash, thrown out of planes, or or or destroyed.　　Some documents were (are) weeded, doctored, butchered, and trimmed are conserved lands/papers are held　　in archives in Berlin, London in foreign homes. I look for my mama in the Berlin wall archive:

Reporter: And do you find it depressing?
Martin Luther King Jr: Yes, I certainly do...

not find mama in the media archives from the wall fall

Reporter: And do you find it depressing?
Martin Luther King Jr: Yes, I certainly do...

Voice *off camera*: Vorsicht!

Berlin, Marienkirche (St. Mary) church September 1964: Let my people go.
We walk past the church every day, I should have placed my ear to the wall
maybe a static from the sermon that Martin Luther King Jr. gave there...
The church is so close to where my brother lives today   sermons his eyes,
when he looks out of his window the knell of the bell rings rings

silence silence silence

form
bent
re-
suspended
returning
wave
or
recipes
on
another
froth

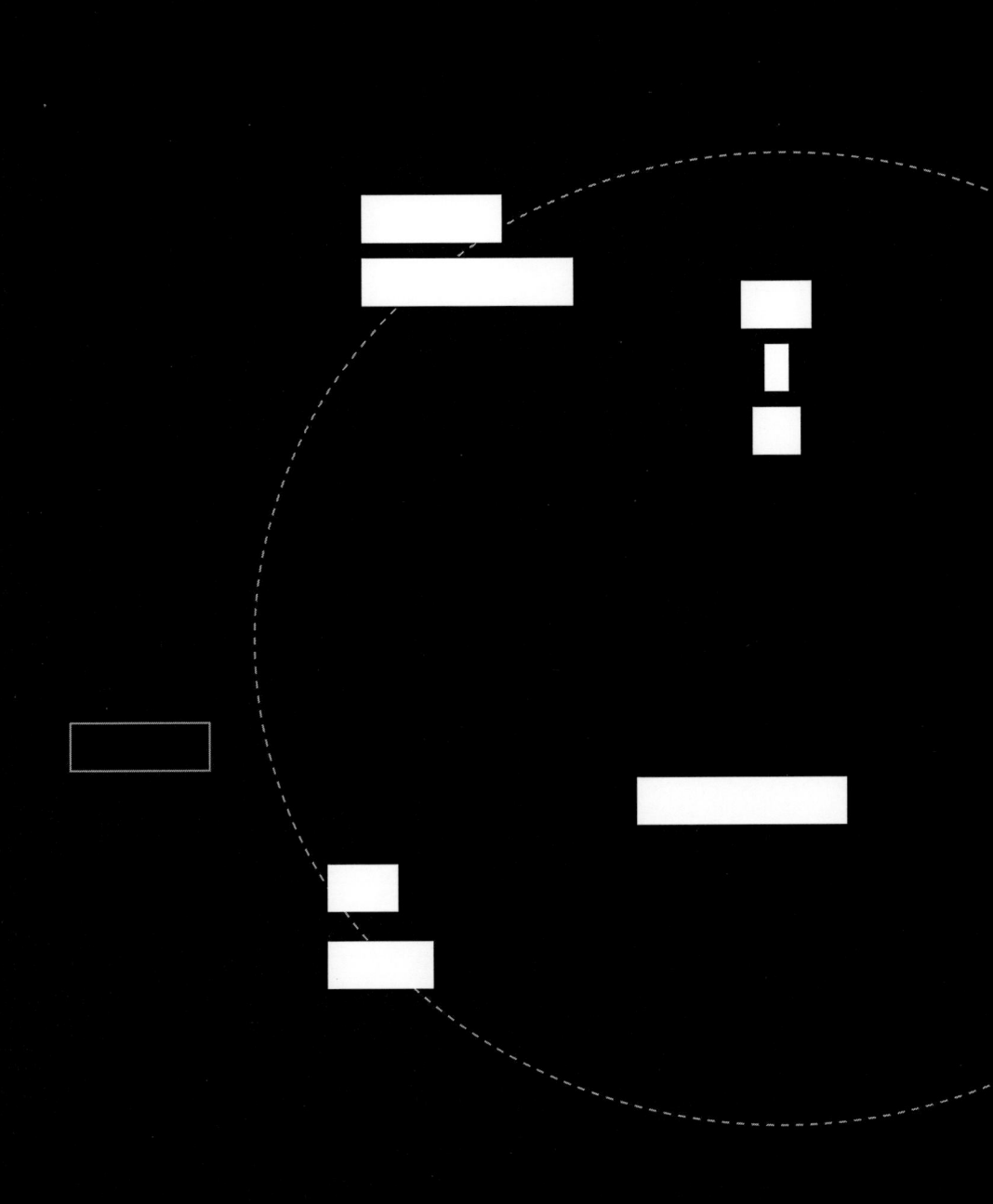

burnt plastic tilts form
the plastic book covers

                                                          sound space

how to arrange the space for sound? I want to make the page a sound

space to listen to. I want the page to perform sound not produce,

through a linguistic, visual, and spatial arrangement. to carry out a

pattern that can be felt, heard, and experienced in the flesh.

the unopened spine bent
inward like a wave curling to
return remaining suspended

mid-air in a cemented gesture of
returning always as the wave
holds onto the half-burnt descriptions, recipes

books sweated in the heat of the flames then wrapped
on to another book becoming one book:
the covers melted into one
another sealed by froth

mama what should I call you now that you are gone?
froth: spirit : marrow : wind

mutter mutter utter utter utter

murmer murmur muma muma mum mummy ma ma ma
mother mother mother
mama

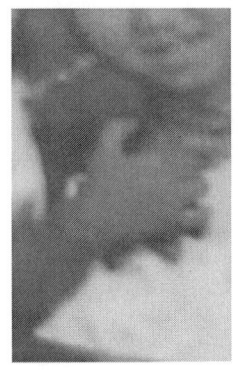

your ashes are not flesh, not blood, not bone
ash : salt : sand :

those are the children with the terminally ill mother

dark blue speckled cup by mama's bedside
pools her saliva pools mama's words

in every city i look for that cup find it and never buy it
hold it to my mouth

spit spit spitting
my story

ACKNOWLEDGMENTS

There are so many people living and otherwise to acknowledge, thank you for all the arrangements that you have all made with me, my poetry, and my words to make this collection possible. First and foremost, I would like to thank my mother Zipora without whose arrangements I would not be here today. Thank you to my teachers, Lyrae Van-Clief Stefanon Leslie A. Adelson, Jacob Sam La-Rose, Ishion Hutchinson, and Rachel Long. Thank you to May Ayim, Raja Lubinetzki, and Audre Lorde, your arrangements with poetry and the earth have made it possible for me to write and continue to imagine and dream.

Asante sanaa, Jumoke Adeyanju for making a space for me and my poetry, for creating Poetry Meets where I first read my poetry in Berlin, and for the love and care that you show me. Thank you to Candice Nembhard, Trovania DeLille, Sailesh Naidu, Natalya Gimson, Juhi. N, Aishwarya. K, and Sakina. H for being my day ones. Thank you, Shenece Oretha for all you are always, for reading the manuscript, thinking with me, for all the poetry poetry poetry, and for the art you make. Thank you to Rhoda Adum Boateng, Chloe Filani, Dove, Hästi Crowther, Olumide Poopola, and my Barbican Young Poets, Obsidian Foundation, and Ledbury Critics Family. Thank you to Gboyega Odubanjo.

Thank you, Aishvarya Arora, for being, and wandering in poetry with me, for reading through the manuscript, and for stopping in front of flowers and trees with me for all you are and always becoming. Thank you to Winniebell Xinyu Zong and Arpita Chakrabarty for the laughter and poetry that you bring into my life. Thank you Ami Tamakloe and Aleah Butler-Jones for your friendship and for listening and being there for all my feelings. Thank you to my brother Joseph Heller, for coming to readings and letting me read to you.

Thank you to public libraries and everyone working in them, special shoutout to the National Poetry Library in London. Thank you to all my ancestors who have dreamt of this book even before I was here. Shukran!

FONO GRAF

1. **Eileen Myles**—*Aloha/irish trees* (LP)

2. **Rae Armantrout**—*Conflation* (LP)

3. **Alice Notley**—*Live in Seattle* (LP)

4. **Harmony Holiday**—*The Black Saint and the Sinnerman* (LP)

5. **Susan Howe & Nathaniel Mackey**—*STRAY: A Graphic Tone* (LP)

6. **Annelyse Gelman & Jason Grier**—*About Repulsion* (EP)

7. **Joshua Beckman**—*Some Mechanical Poems To Be Read Aloud* (print)

8. **Dao Strom**—*Instrument/ Traveler's Ode* (print; cassette tape)

9. **Douglas Kearney & Val Jeanty**—*Fodder* (LP)

10. **Mark Leidner**—*Returning the Sword to the Stone* (print)

11. **Charles Valle**—*Proof of Stake: An Elegy* (print)

12. **Emily Kendal Frey**—*LOVABILITY* (print)

13. **Brian Laidlaw and the Family Trade**—*THIS ASTER: adaptations of Emile Nelligan* (LP)

14. **Nathaniel Mackey and The Creaking Breeze Ensemble**—*Fugitive Equation* (compact disc)

15. *FE Magazine* (print)

16. **Brandi Katherine Herrera**—*MOTHER IS A BODY* (print)

17. **Jan Verberkmoes**—*Firewatch* (print)

18. **Krystal Languell**—*Systems Thinking with Flowers* (print)

19. **Matvei Yankelevich**—*Dead Winter* (print)

20. **Cody-Rose Clevidence**—*Dearth & God's Green Mirth* (print)

21. **Hilary Plum**—*Hole Studies* (print)

22. **John Ashbery**—*Live at Sanders Theatre, 1976* (LP)

23. **Alice Notley**—*The Speak Angel Series* (print)

24. **Alice Notley**—*Early Works* (print)

25. **Joshua Marie Wilkinson**—*Trouble Finds You* (print)

26. **Timmy Straw**—*The Thomas Salto* (print)

27. **Audre Lorde**—*At Fassett Studio, 1970* (LP)

28. **Gabriel Palacios**—*A Ten Peso Burial For Which Truth I Sign* (print)

29. **Isabel Zapata, trans. Robin Myers**—*A Whale Is a Country* (print)

30. **Callum Angus**—*Cataract* (print)

31. **Eds. Dao Strom & Jyothi Natarajan**—*FE/De-Canon Anthology* (print)

32. **Cody-Rose Clevidence**—*The Grimace of Eden, Now* (print)

33. **Jaydra Johnson**—*Low: Notes on Art and Trash* (print)

34. **Jaime Gil de Biedma**—*If Only For a Moment (I'll Never Be Young Again)* (print)

Fonograf Editions is a registered 501(c)(3) nonprofit organization. Find more information about the press at: fonografeditions.com.